"I have fallen in love with Melly's new enlightening and inspiring look at the stag woman might grow through as she becomes more conscious.

Growth is often uncomfortable and sometimes painful. I felt both seen and heard, validated and healed, as I recognised the stages of my own personal journey in Melly's words. And I knew that it was perfectly ok to choose to be in my power. Thank you for your wisdom, Melly, and for creating such a beautiful space in which to explore all that we can be."

Deborah Fay – Counsellor | Author | Publisher @ *Disruptive Publishing*

"WOW. I am 51 years of age and have been waiting for this book all my life. The read is truly profound. The words reaching inside of me and bring me out. My original spiritual awakening was at 25 years and I've been on this path since. This book, this magic, this art, this extraordinary experience is my new spiritual awakening. I feel fearless, I feel ready and I love you Melly. I encourage you all to venture in. The forest is green, clean, refreshing and beckoning you to enter. Enter safely with the gentle and beautiful soul – Melly. She will help you, she will hold your space for you, until you can do it for yourself. A must read for all of us. Women join our circle."

Katrena Friel – Author | Speaker | Business Mentor @ *Becoming the Expert*

ABOUT MELLY STEWART

Melly Stewart is the author of *Stages of Self: Your Journey to Self-Empowerment*, a poetically written framework showing women how to break the cycles of disempowerment and pain embedded in their lives. As a Women's Personal and Business Development Mentor, she takes women who are ignoring their own needs due to the pressures of everyday life from overwhelmed and unsure, to a confident woman boldly walking through life in the direction of their dreams. Through Melly's Training, Facilitation, Keynote Presentations, and Intuitive Tarot Readings she takes spiritually minded women through their own *Stages of Self* showing everyone that Personal *or* Business... it all starts with *you*.

www.mellys.com.au

MELLY STEWART

STAGES *of* *Self*

YOUR JOURNEY TO
SELF-EMPOWERMENT

ISBN: #978-0-6489671-8-7

My Lexi,

May these pages serve you,

And all other sensitive souls like you,

To reclaim the power of who you truly are

My darling girl,

It is that big open heart of yours that makes your smile so warm and inviting

It is that inquisitive mind of yours that make your eyes twinkle with curiosity

It is that vibrant sensitivity to life itself that makes your soul so magnetic

But my darling girl,

I have watched that smile disappear from your face with words that cut deep

I have watched that twinkle fade from your eyes from the actions of others

I have watched your soul retreat to protect itself from the pain of this world

And my darling girl,

My heart aches watching those lips remain silent

My heart aches watching those eyes fill with tears

My heart aches watching yours break into a million pieces.

Oh but my darling girl!

The day will come when you finally scream enough

The day will come when you finally claim back your power

The day will come when you finally realise the truth

And on that day my darling girl...

That's when you will discover you are magical.

Contents

13... Forward

17... Tools to Support You

21... The Princess

55... The Mother Goddess

101... The Wild Woman

175... The Dark Queen

277... The Sorceress

335... Stepping Forward

337... About the Author

339... Thank-you

Forward

There is a story that all women instinctively know. A story that lies deep within our hearts and was once passed down from mother to daughter, all throughout the ages. But at some point in history, this story was put under lock and key.

Exactly why, no one truly knows, and at this point in time, the reason behind its suppression has become irrelevant. What IS relevant, is our responsibility to do something about the consequences of keeping this story locked within us.

You see, this story that was not passed down…

This story that lies deep within us…

…is the story of the cycles that all woman experience. (And I don't mean the menstrual one we are taught about in a sex-ed video at school.)

I'm talking about the story of the *emotional* cycles that are the pathway to our true magnetic empowerment.

The cycles that are the pathway to our magic.

This is the story that our mothers didn't know they had to teach us. The story that *their* mothers didn't know they had to teach *them*. The story that has been forgotten over time and left generation after generation of women, chasing their tails trying to figure out what the 'wrong' feeling is within themselves.

Because while this is the story of our empowerment, it is also the story of what happens when these emotional cycles are not addressed.

It is also the story of our disempowerment.

The story of how we have ALLOWED ourselves to become depressed, weakened, damaged, deprived, day after day, generation after generation. Not at the hand of others…

…but by our own.

Stages of Self is about bringing that story to light so we can end the deep inherent pain embedded in all women. The deep inherent pain that we feel so deeply physically, mentally, spiritually and in turn, emotionally. The pain that we are trying so hard to run away from.

It's about providing a pathway for women to find the self-awareness required to view their own story with clear eyes. Then, with radical self-love, face the cycles of shame that are keeping them trapped in their pain and holding them back from self-empowerment. But more than that, its about finding the courage to take responsibility for what they will do once they have transformed this pain into power.

And here's the thing…

When a woman makes the commitment to go through these cycles with self-awareness, radical self-love and courage, she sets the foundation for those around her to do the same. She becomes a beacon of strength and by her simple magnetic presence, teaches others what it means to be an empowered woman, living a life of magic, in honour of herself.

So the fact you have this book in your hands right now, is a sign that you are ready. You are ready to take the first steps to ending the cycles of disempowerment within yourself that have been passed down from generation to generation.

Whether you are beginning this journey because of your children, your nieces, your mother, your partner, your friend or even your business… ultimately the reason you are beginning is irrelevant. Because no matter where your journey begins, it *will* come back to you.

This is *your* choice.

Your life.

Your responsibility to *yourself.*

This is where *you* draw the line in the sand and say…

Universe,

Hear me now.

This pain stops with me.

Right here.

Right now.

It is time to unlock the path before me.

When I get lost, light my way in the dark.

Show me the truth hiding under my illusions.

Banish this pain from my heart,

Once and for all.

I am ready for my journey to begin.

I am ready to know my

Stages of Self.

Tools to Support You

My vision is so much bigger than this book. My goal is to provide the support, guidance, and education that all women are missing so, together, we can master our emotional cycles and find our way to self-empowerment. Here are some of the way you may find that support:

#courage1000project Podcast & WebTV

Listen to the weekly #courage1000project podcast for women who are seeking the courage to take the next steps in their life or business.

Darling You Are Magical Community

Join a community of women who are all working on developing the confidence to move forward in life and/or business. Every Monday 9am AEST, join me LIVE for a Weekly Energy Update + Exclusive Community Offer plus regular updates on all things Stages of Self.

Discover Your Stages of Self - Quiz & Free Download

Are you a Princess? Maybe a Mother Goddess? Or are you the deep and mysterious Dark Queen? Find out what Stage of Self you are in with the free online quiz and then download the Archetype cheat sheet to get a better understanding. Please share your revelations by using the hashtag #stagesofself on any of your favourite social media platforms and let's start a movement of women standing in their power.

www.MellyS.com.au

What if your story got to start again

And those times you were told no, never happened?

How magical would life be if your freedom

To be who you are, was never taken away?

#mellysthestorycollector

She dances through the fields

Gracefully carefree

As quickly as the wind changes

So to her direction

Forever dancing

Moving

In her search for adventure

Her heart called for freedom

Movement

Independence

She wanted to run

Where her heart wished to go

No thought

No holding back

A life fully expressed

On the edge of danger

Excitement

Expansion

Life was big

And she wanted to taste it all

Wanting more options

But less decisions

Wanting more adventure

But less risk

Wanting more independence

But less responsibility

She just wanted more

Out of life

Out of herself

Out of the world

With her eyes always on the horizon

They worried she would float away

So they tied cement blocks to her feet

Wrapped her up tightly in their rules

Under the pretence

That this was 'for her best'

'Be a good girl'

They said

'But don't be a pushover'

'You are in control'

They said

'But do as your told'

'Be educated'

They said

'But not too smart for your own good'

'You are a woman now'

They said

'But don't talk about your sexuality'

'Speak up'

They said

'But keep your opinion to yourself'

'Be unique'

They said

'But make sure you fit in with everyone else'

'Stand up for yourself'

They said

'But don't be a bossy bitch'

'Be strong'

They said

'But not too strong, its unattractive'

'Be sexy'

They said

'But don't dress like a slut'

Confusion clouded her thoughts

As their words stretched her mind

Pulling it   apart   piece   b y   p i e c   e

How can I follow their rules

When each contradicts the one before?

How many more I am to learn?

And when do I get to make my own?

I don't care about your rules

Or commitments

Expectations

Regulations

I want to dance

Unruly and free

I want to be me

When do I get to be me?

Pushed aside under the guise

Of being too different

Excluded by her peers

Isolated for not following the rules

Which were tearing her mind apart

Simply because she still dared to fly

The tears streamed down her face

"Why are they so mean to me?"

"My darling," Mother whispered

"They want what you have.

That light in your heart.

But because they can't find it within themselves

And they can't figure out how to get it on their own,

They will settle for destroying yours instead."

Where do I belong?

I don't fit anywhere

Not with my family

Not with my friends

Forever an outsider

Looking in on my life

A stranger in my own body

She felt like a bird

With b
      r
        o
          k
            e
              n
                wings

Constricted

Restricted

No longer   whole

Desperate

To fly away

Desperate

To be free

The weight of the world

Dropped on her shoulders

Forced upon her

Without her consent

And for no other reason

Then the same had been done to them

Heart breaking

Eyes stinging

Freedom lost

Too vulnerable

Too open

Too raw

Forced to hide behind a mask

Covering the pain

From a world that did not care

Heart turned to stone

Eyes turned to daggers

Words became weapons

In the war for her freedom

If the only way to get freedom

Was to burn everything down

Then so be it

She would pour gasoline

Strike a match

And watch the world burn

Go ahead

Tell me what to do

Then watch me walk away

Middle finger in the air

She was now a bomb

Ready to explode

Ready to throw her anger

Her resentment

Her pain

At anyone within her reach

Made from the chains of their restrictions

Fuelled by the weight of their expectations

With one lick of flame

She would destroy everything in her path

Even if it meant destroying herself

I just want somebody to save me

To make it all go away

The fear

The pain

The uncertainty

I don't want to do this anymore

Somebody fix this for me.

She knew they were not good for her

With their beautiful words

Falling like silk on her skin

Nothing but sweet lies

A ploy

A tactic

To uncover the wetness

Between her legs

But she didn't care

She wanted the attention

To feel seen

To be wanted

She wanted everything she could not have

Was not allowed to have

So she encouraged them to desire her

With the bat of her eyelashes

And a wiggle of her hips

And waited eagerly

For their beautiful words

That fell like silk on her skin

Why do I keep waiting for you?

To wake up

To see me

To rescue me from my pain

Why do I keep hurting myself

With the agony of my own anger

Waiting for something that is never going to come?

I will not be a casualty of my own pain

I am not waiting for you any longer

I will rescue myself

Palms sweaty

Trembling voice

She stood her ground

While her whole world shook

Her eyes darted around

Seeking acknowledgment

Longing to be seen

For what she had accomplished

But nobody had noticed

They were all too busy

Looking for acknowledgement of their own

Did you ever see me?

Turns out you didn't.

You couldn't.

Because you were still waiting for somebody to see you.

What if she'd been blaming the wrong people this whole time?

What if it was never them?

What if it was always her?

She was not a child anymore.

Her feelings.

Her needs.

They were her responsibility.

It was up to her to look after herself.

I'm not bound to you.

You are not a cement block

Tied to my ankles.

But if I release myself from this false belief

What stops me from floating away?

What if she stopped restricting herself?

Setting terms

And limits

Adhering to their structures

And their rules

What if she said No.

What if she gave herself permission to just be?

I will no longer second guess myself

Or blindly follow the rules of the past

I refuse to be part of your cycle of pain

Or tie myself to your beliefs

I've waited long enough

To follow my heart

It's time to live my life

My way

By my choices

Not by yours

And the truth had set her free

It was her life

It was her responsibility

She needed no permission

To be herself

The doors of her future had flung wide open

Her path an open field to explore once more

She danced through the fields again

Gracefully carefree

And now when the wind changed

It was her choice to follow

Forever free

To choose

The path of her adventure

Seen by the only person who mattered

…Herself

Nothing truly prepares you for stepping into your Nurturer

It is a bittersweet irony of the best and worst of life

Walking together side by side

In the cavities of your heart

#mellysthestorycollector

She cried out in pain

Her mind a tumble of confusion

Body aching

Heart breaking

Soul weary

She wanted someone to hold her

To tell her it was going to be ok

That this was a bad dream

But she knew in her heart

These words would be lies

A part of her was breaking

Transforming

Transitioning

Rebirthing into something new

Her heart was expanding

Breaking

Fusing

Twisting

Morphing

Uncovering the centre

Where the depth of her love lay

Dormant

Inactive

But begging to be released

So while her body ached

Her heart broke

Her soul grew weary

She knew this was a gift

For she was on the edge of motherhood

Not in body

But in spirit

She wiped their tears

Held their fears

Embraced their hearts

And by her caring kiss

Let love be known

She saw potential

In the eyes of a child

In the whisper of an idea

In the unspoken words of a conversation

So many unassuming moments of promise

And although she did not know how

She vowed to help these seeds of life grow

Like an umbrella

Shielding those beneath it

She too tried to protect those in her care

Unawares

They were longing to feel the rain

Why do they push me away?

I'm trying to help them live

To grow strong and protected

Free of the pain I experienced

Why do they reject me?

Why do they hurt my heart so?

Her intentions

Once pure

Unrecognisable from before

As they TwiStED

Within her

Consumed by her need to be needed

She reached out for love

Only to be rejected

Another arrow to her heart

If they did not give their love freely

She would take it by force

So she used her words

Her emotions

Her actions

To sway the world around her

Until all those in her life knew

Without her

They would have nothing

Until all those around her believed

Without her

They were nothing

I have no idea what I am doing

But I try repeatedly

Day

After day

One step

After the other

I give

And I give

Over

And over again

And yet

No matter what I do

Its just not good enough

I'm not good enough

Im

Not

Good

Enough

For

You

She wrapped her heart in armour

Made access payable in favour

'Show me you love me

Then I'll show you I love you'

She had weaponised her love

Controlling others with scorn

Disappointment

Disapproval

Withholding love from all and any

Who failed her impossible tests

She bound them to her

With barbed wire

Dripping with the blood of their pain

Unawares

It was dripping with her blood too

Just love me

Is that such a big ask?

Love me for cooking for our family

Love me for keeping our house clean

Love me for running after our children

Love me for carrying the weight of a thousand things

On my shoulders

On my hips

In my mind

In my heart

Love me for doing this

Is that too much to ask?

>   *....Why can't I say these words to you?*

She was losing herself

Piece by piece

In between the routines

The schedules

The requests

That were not her own

The chaotic monotony

Of motherhood

Began eating her alive

I'm empty

I have nothing left to give

So why do you keep asking for more?

Although she loved those she cared for

Ever so deeply

It was too much to take

She needed space

To be

To feel

To allow herself the numbness

Slowly creeping into her heart

Space was a luxury she did not have

Quiet an elegance she could not afford

Independence now seemed foreign and strange

She did the only thing she knew

Would truly numb the pain

        …And opened another bottle

Life had become an unstable game

Of emotional roulette

Would she become the firestorm

Destroying everything in her path?

Would she become the tsunami

And wash everyone away with her tears?

Or worse yet

Would she become the earthquake

And break their very foundations apart?

She lived everyday

Tiptoeing the line

Between sanity

And despair

Never finding the courage

To voice how dark

Some days truly felt

I feel too much

In a world that doesn't feel at all

Am I broken?

Or is the world?

Conviction in her voice

Image reflecting in the mirror

'I am not my emotions' she said

Her mind screamed in protest

'Oh but you are!

You ARE an explosion waiting to happen.'

Her heart whispered in confusion

'But I don't mean it!

I'm just exhausted from everything I do for them.'

Her mind screamed back

'And yet you hurt them over and over again

How could anyone love you?'

Her heart cried out in pain

'How can you be so cruel?

I don't deserve to be treated like this!'

As the war raged on within

Head vs heart

Tears gauged canyons

In the lines of her tired face

What if by numbing the pain

I'm numbing out other feelings too?

What if I'm blocking myself from love?

Tears drying on her cheeks

She stared at the woman in the mirror

And said the words she had been longing to hear

"I love you."

So she stopped

Stopped resisting the pain

Stopped blocking it out

Numbing it out

Wishing it away

She let it flood in

Drown her in emotions

Drown her in feeling

Consuming her

Overtaking her

She stopped

Stopped being in control

Stopped being strong

Holding tightly

Pushing it away

And let it all in

For a moment

An ever-so brief moment

Time

Stood

Still

The future

Non-existent

The past

No longer relevant

In the stillness

Of the now

With all emotion drained

Her senses heightened

Feeling and sensing life

Like she never had before

Grass tapping at her fingertips

Wind gently kissing her skin

Sunlight softly warming her back

The world around her

Above her

Under her

Holding her in her pain

Comforting her

Supporting her

Deep breathes of gratitude

Inhaling the love

The earth had to give

Mother Earth I hear you,

Behind the noise

The busy-ness of the world

I hear you

A hum

A purr

Your heartbeat

And when I block out the world

That sound

That vibration

Is like warm kisses on my skin

Like being wrapped in the arms of the one I love

You are love

I am loved

I love you

As freely as the earth

Gave its love to her

She knew she could love again

Completely

Eagerly

Unconditionally

To love means to be open

To joy and happiness

To wonder and excitement

But love has two sides

Just like a coin

To love means to be open

To heartache and disappointment

To hurt and grief

But both are necessary

For love to exist

She would no longer fear

The cracking of her heart

Or the onslaught of emotions

For each time her heart broke

Her tears glued it back together

Stronger than before

And so began the difficult task

Learning to love herself

While she was busy

Loving others

The curve of her hips

Her lips

Her thighs

The softness of her face

Her breasts

Her stomach

The unpredictability of her tears

Her smiles

Her hugs

The things which once made her cringe

Now made her laugh with glee

For she realised her imperfections

Made her perfectly feminine

And how could there be any flaws

In a woman's sensuality?

I am worthy

And deserving

Of love

From others

I am worthy

And deserving

Of love

From the world

But most importantly

I am worthy

And deserving

Of love

From myself

Even at my worst

In order to give herself space

To love herself the way she deserved

She had to love and nurture others so deeply

As to foster their independence

But this was the irony of motherhood

In order to create a future

Where she was no longer needed

She had to love them more

By loving them less

You stand before me

Tears streaming down your face

My Princess

My child

"It's just not fair!"

You scream between sobs

I want to take away your pain

Grab you in a bear hug

Hold you close

Breathe in your scent

Absorb your hurt into me

Just as I did

When you were my baby

I want to say to you

"Yes. You're right.

It's their fault."

But I know this won't help you

Allowing you to be a victim

Giving away your power

Belittling your confidence

With each portion of blame you throw

Instead I take a deep breath

Forcing back the desire

To sweep you into my arms

I grab you by the shoulders

Stare deep into your eyes

"Yes. Sometimes life is not fair.

But you always have a choice...

Complain or do something about it.

What choice will you make?

Will you choose to stay in your pain?

Or will you choose to walk through it?"

Inside world pushing outwards

Expanding

Clawing

Dragging its way to the surface

She needed space to process

This feeling

This emotion

This thing within her that she could not name

The tears flowed freely

Unapologetically

Without restraint

Or even the slightest hint of remorse

Her emotions flowed

Simply because they must

Simply because

This was a woman's way

The tears flowed down her cheeks

As her heart asked her to feel

And she had been through too much

To ever deny her heart again

I love my tears

They show me I am filled

With compassion and kindness

I love my body

For it provides nurturing space

To those who need it

I love my heart

Which is wide open

To experience all that life

Has to offer

The good

The bad

And all the shades in between

And I adore that I get to feel it all

One tear at a time

There is something truly beautiful

About a woman who shows her emotions

Who lets them flow unhindered

By the restraints and expectations of everyday life

Her heart was wide open now

Which made it easier to break

And break it did

A little more each and every day

Gluing itself back together

Each and every time

Stronger

Firmer

Bigger

With the love that radiated from within her

A continual process

Opening

Breaking

Loving

A never-ending journey of perpetual heart expansion

There is something so confident and strong

In the women with messy hair and mismatched clothes

The ones who speak to animals and hug the trees

Maybe it is that wild glint in their eyes

#mellysthestorycollector

The dark forest stood before her

Brooding

Heaving

Whispering

What lay behind her

While filled with love and joy

Now seemed hollow

Shallow

Empty

She had spent many seasons

Tendering

Nurturing

Helping others grow

Gifting them independence

But something new was emerging

Asking her to shed her skin

To leave the essence of the Mother Goddess behind

The need to run had returned

But not like before

This was different

She was not running away from responsibility

She was running towards herself

Towards something deeper

Towards something she could not yet comprehend

Towards a secret that whispered on the wind

And hung in the air around her

So by the silvery light of the full moon

As her clothes hit the grass beneath her feet

She stepped forward into the dark forest

Naked

Raw

Willingly

Into the mystery of the unknown

The true language of the earth could be heard

In the stillness of the trees

Whispers of her ancient history

Within the birds song

Within the rustle of the leaves

Within the distant sound of running water

Here

The earths voice rang

Quiet and clear

A constant hum

In the back of her mind

And in this stillness

Comforted by the earths voice

She found home

A new rhythm to life

Was found

One that was slower

More deliberate

Then the stages before

She found peace

In the solitude

Of the forest

The wild was intoxicating

She was forgetting herself

In the silence

In that hum between sound

Succumbing to the comfort

Of her true nature

She let the Wild Woman within

Roam free

She could feel its pull

The delicious taste of ecstasy

Beckoning her forward

Deeper into the moonlit woods

Here she could sense the depth of life

Feel the soul of the earth itself

And she delighted in the pleasure

That it mirrored her own

For the night

    The forest

        The moon

            It was wild

                …And so was she

I have the time I have always wanted

The space that I have craved

The freedom to do as I please

But what do I do with it

Now that I have it?

There were dreams

Desires

Needs

Wants

Locked within her

Things never realised

Not the right time

Right moment

Right place

But now

She held the key in her hands

And wondered what would happen

If she dared to open the lock

She wanted more again

But not of life

Of herself

More awareness

More understanding

More depth

She wanted to know more

About who she was

Underneath everything

She had become

I release the need to be

What others want me to be

And accept the need to be

What I want me to be

But what is it that I want?

She knew finding her truth was more

Then searching through her memories

It was an excavation of self

An unravelling of her beliefs

And she had to keep going

No matter where it took her

Because

Just like the moon

Nothing could stay hidden forever

How had I forgotten

The things that I longed to be?

Those dreams that were started

But never completed

Why had I never chased them?

Why had I never fought for them?

Why had I given them up so easily?

Lost in a forest of memories

Each knocking on the door in her mind

Asking her to remember

Re-live

Review

The choices she made

The moments that hurt

Things not yet forgiven

Moments from her life

Now lumps of coal within her

Dirty

Crumbling

Retaining heat

Ready to reignite

You took something that didn't belong to you

Something that was never yours to take

And you let a young woman believe

She was nothing more than meat

Why did I let you?

Why did I let you take my power away?

There was a power in her emotions

In the tears she shed

In the love she gave

Power in her softness and vulnerability

And the way she readily gave it away

There was a power in her curves

In the shape of her lips

In the curve of her hips

Power in the space between her legs

And the way she bled red

Yet they convinced her this was dirty

That the power of her sensuality

The gift of femininity

And the most fundamental element of her identity

Was wrong

And their words and actions cut deep

As time and time again

They tried to remove her power

The gift of womanhood

"I'm paying for it." He had said

"So you have to go get it."

Within an instant

A millennium of feminine oppression

Crash tackled her entire being

Echoes of the past rising to the surface

"I'm paying for it." They had said

"So do my bidding."

And within an instant

Women became slaves to a mans will

"I'm paying for it." They had said

"So get on your knees."

And within an instant

Women's bodies were no longer their own

"I'm paying for it." They had said.

"So you don't need to worry about it."

And within an instance

Women's intuitions were shut down

"I'm paying for it." They had said

"So you get what you're given."

And within an instant

Women's choices were taken away

"I'm paying for it." He had said

Ever so harmlessly that day

"So you have to go get it."

But the echoes of the past

Haunted her

Forever etched into her heart

Her memories ate at her

Biting and chewing into her beating heart

Until she realised

That was why she covered it in armour in the first place

Our power comes

From knowing who we are

But you denied me of this

Just as your parents had done to you

And their parents before them

Generation after generation

Of denial, suppression, and repression

Blackmailed and abused

Into keeping my strength locked up inside

Brainwashed and convinced

That this was for my best

And that I should be grateful for your love

Grateful to be allowed to love you

What was I thinking?

Why did I let your pain dictate my life?

The heat of a thousand suns

Began to burn deep within her

Fuelling

Fanning

The rising flames of rage

With each memory of power lost

Anger sunk deeper

Growing bitter and twisted

Chaos scratching at her insides

Begging to be released

She had spent her life being the hunted

Forever the potential prey

Of those seeking power and control

And as the wild woman's bitterness grew

She picked up her dagger

And vowed no one would ever hurt her again

Fuck you!

Fuck the world!

I won't let anybody

Take my power away again.

I will wear this armour

Day and night

Forever prepared

Forever ready

For the day you attack

Again

Even though it made her strong

Fierce

Unstoppable

In the face of the battle

As time went on

With each fight she fought

Her armour grew thicker

Harder to carry

But she refused to put it down

For it also kept the world around her

Safe

Protected

From the twisted anger

Forcing its way to the surface of her skin

Over time

Even a feather

Held onto too tightly

Will bear the weight of a rock

I'm tired of trying harder

I'm tired of burning up from the inside

It's all too hard

Too heavy

Too hot

Molten in my head and heart

Its time to let it burn

Until there is nothing left but ashes

But will this burn me too?

Will there be anything left of me afterwards?

She was tired of wearing her armour

Tired of carrying the weight of hate

Tired of protecting herself

Tired of holding the chaos inside

Her body ached to let it go

To release it all

To set herself free

From the weight

Of her own anger

The sound escaping her lips

Was primal

Raw

Unnerving

Scaring her

At how much anger

How much pain

Had been locked within her over time

That fear drove the sound even deeper

Louder

Stronger

A deathly

Bone chilling sound

Forcing the world to stillness

Fearful of enduring the wrath being unleashed

She screamed from the depths of her soul

Until her throat ached

Voice cracking

Hands shaking

Her body no longer supporting the weight of her rage

Giving way beneath her

Falling to the forest floor

She pounded her fists

Into the soft earth

Tearing

Clawing

At anything within her reach

Destroying anything in her path

Chaos personified

In the body of a woman

With the sound of her own heartbeat

Throbbing in her ears

Her chest rising and falling

As each breath slowed and deepened

Slowly

Ever so slowly

The rage subsided

And a voice of wisdom began to rise

Step back from your pain

Look at yourself

See what you have become

A jolt of electricity to her heart

Terror at the person she was turning into

Witnessing her own destruction

Tears now filling the space

Where the weight of her anger once lived

Tears of exhaustion

Relief

Sadness

Grief

Great heaving sobs

Releasing all the feelings of pain

Of powerlessness

Of sadness

Of hurt

Of every single feeling

That had wrapped itself up

In the chaos of her bitterness

The tears fell heavy

Until the storm within

Had lost its ferocity

Leaving nothing

But silent space behind

As she lay in the naked earth

Surrounded by her destruction

Get up, Little One.

You are not broken

Your journey is not over

Allow the flames of your rage

To empower your spirit

And rise from the ashes

Like the phoenix you are

Never to doubt your strength again

What is this voice?

Where is it coming from?

Why does it sound strong

When I feel so weak?

We are the ones who have walked

This path before

In our own way

In our own time

Holding our own pain

We are the ones they called Heretic

Witch

Hag

For we chose this path

And left the herd of men behind

We are the Wild Women of your ancestry

And our wisdom

Our knowing

Our strength

Runs deep within your blood

Little One,

We stand behind you

Beside you

Within you

Always

In the quiet void

Now clear of emotion

The naked earth beneath her

Her heartbeat steadying

Her entire body throbbed

Acute awareness

Of the blood within her

Pulsating just beneath the skin

I'm done

I've burned myself up

From the inside out

There is nothing but ash

Running through my veins

I am a hollow echo

Of what once was

Leave me be

Allow me the stillness

The peace

As I wait for the wind

To carry me away

This you must know,

You are born of the fire

Your strength is forged in the fire

And it is your turn to dance in the flames

Get up Little One!

Rise from the ashes

Of your own destruction

Claim the Phoenix within you!

Soul aching

Mind empty

Body numb

Shaking hands

Shallow breathing

Unsteady feet

Rising from the dirt

The strength of the earth

The strength of her ancestors

Rising with her

Let our wisdom grow

Deepen

Settle within you

Allow us to guide you forward

Follow our sacred path

Keep going

One foot in front of the other

I don't know where this will go

But there is nothing left behind

Except destruction and pain

So I will keep moving forward

One foot in front of the other

I will follow you

Fragments of armour

Littered the path before her

And the visions

Of woman on their knees

Tearing

Clawing

At the earth beneath them

Began to fill her mind

The sound of their bone chilling cry

Hanging in the air

Like a spectral trapped in time

The final resting places

Of a woman's rage

There have been so many of us

Who have found ourselves

In this forest

So many of us

Bearing the weight of rage

So many of us

Who let their chaos free

Along the edges of this path

But what happened to them?

What happened when the rose from the dirt?

Will I discover it too?

Every secret waits for its time to be called out

And there are secrets within you

A knowledge

A wisdom

Ancient

True

Powerful

Hidden under the anger

You have held within for so long

Hidden within the wants

Needs

Desires

Of your life

It's time to let them free

Those things kept under lock and key for so long

Once more began stirring within her

It had taken time

But she was ready now

            …She turned the key

I'm not breaking anymore

I'm no longer fragile

I'm learning

I'm growing

I'm evolving

And although I have no idea where I'm going

Or what lies ahead

I know I am supported

By all those who walked before me

And that is enough

To keep me moving forward

The ghosts of the past

Danced beneath the treetops

Following her along the path

Whispering their wisdom

As lightly as the wind

Kissing the leaves

She realised these ghosts

The ancients of her past

Had always been with her

They had walked beside her

All her life

In the books she had read

In the movies she had watched

In the tales her mother told

They had always been with her

But blinded by her hidden rage

The wisdom they were trying to share

Had not been heard

But here

As she walked the path before her

She could hear it clearly

And welcomed it into her heart

You made your mark in history

And left it right where I could see

But because it was so obvious

I mistook it for the mundane

But I see it now

I see the magic you have woven

Into the world

To help me

Guide me

Support me

You have always been there for me

Hidden in the everyday existence

Of life itself

I'm sorry it took me so long to realise

Thank-you for being patient with me

But most importantly

I love you for everything you have done

All of you

They taught her how to read

The signs guiding her way

In the eyes of the animals

That crossed her path

In the scent of the flowers

That grew on its edges

In the ancient symbols

Carved into the trees

In the stacked rocks and twigs

Placed ever so carefully

Each time she felt lost

The next sign would be waiting for her

Guiding her along

The wild woman's sacred path

All these symbols

Animals

Synchronicities

Pointing to one thing

The silvery moon hanging above my head

Why?

Grandmother Moon reminds us

Even in our darkest nights

When her light is gone

And we feel the depths of our emotions

Will swallow us whole

That there is always hope

Of the new approaching

For the moon never stays dark

Grandmother Moon reminds us

That there will be times

When her light is bright

And we feel ourselves energetically expanding

Out into the world

To rejoice in the lightness

Of this feeling

For the moon never stays full

Grandmother Moon reminds us

Of the inherent power

Born in the natural cycles

Of the wax and wane

For it is the power within that cycle

Which guides the ocean

To retreat from the land

Or to gently kiss its shores

Grandmother Moon reminds us

By her mere presence

Each and every night

That the cyclical sway of our emotions

The natural ebb and flow

Embedded into our hearts

Locked into our very existence

Is the story of all women

Each and every night

The moon began whispering

Fragments of information

Dancing behind her eyelids

Dreams too strange to comprehend

Yet the emotions left behind

Upon the rising of the sun

Could not be mistaken

This knowledge within her

So complicated to hear

But its messages simple

Light

Feather like

If she grabbed at it too tightly

Allowed her anger to take over in frustration

It disintegrated in her hands

To retrieve it she must be patient

Soft yet strong

A container for it to fall into

She must allow it to reveal itself

Grandmother Moon,

Help me please.

Help me unlock the space within me

So that I may understand your messages

Help light my way in the dark

So that I do not get lost in my own emotions

Pierce my illusions with your knowing

So that I may flow with you

Forever more

The Moon was full

When she heard the call

Drumbeats echoing

From within her own heartbeat

Thump thump

Thump thump

Enchanted by the sound

Following it blindly

Through the moonlit forest

Letting the ancients of her past

Lead the way

The chant of the Wild Woman

Her ancestors

Her guides

Reverberated within her

As she walked

Their voices singing loud and clear

The kindness and strength in their unity

Filling her with hope

Energy

Excitement

The drew her to a clearing

Deep within the forest

Well protected by the trees

And she watched in awe

As the ghosts of the past

Came to life

Under the beams of moonlight

Caressing the earth

She gifts us all

With the awareness we are seeking

When we are ready

To open our minds

Our hearts

Our bodies

To her completely

With Mother Earth below

And Grandmother Moon above

In our nakedness

Our freedom

Our ecstasy

Her messages become clear

Come, Little One

It's time to embrace her gift

And so they danced

Naked

Freely

Wildly

Unapologetic and unrestrained

In their bodies

Voices

Emotions

Feeling everything merge into one

The earth

The night

The elements

Until they no longer knew where they ended

And the rest of the world began

Do you see now, Little One?

Do you understand?

Have you heard her message?

Do you embrace her gift?

Yes!

It is not about looking

Or thinking

Or hearing

Or smelling

Its deeper than that

I must feel

Feel what is under me

Around me

Part of me

When I feel this deeply

I connect to the ancient part of myself

My primal nature

The part of me that knows

What my conscious mind

Cannot comprehend

It is here

In the most primal part of myself

That something new is forming

This is your path now

You do not need us to lead you anymore

But we will always be with you

In the wind

In the stars

In the moon

In the eyes of an animal

In the feather floating in the air

We will always be with you

Should you ever need to access

Our collective wisdom

Morning sun

Warming her skin

Eyes heavy

Heart full

Soul light

Feeling the renewed strength

Blazing quietly within her

She could easily lose herself

To the Wild Woman within

Let herself forever roam free

In the comfort of the forest

Dancing naked under the moon

Running with the animals

Allowing herself to feel all of life

At its most extreme depth

But her heart told her there was more

Her journey did not end here

It was only just beginning

Her whole life had been spent searching

Seeking answers to a question not fully formed

Always at the tip of her tongue

But never spoken out loud

Eventually locked deep within

A safe place to keep the whisper

Ready for the day

When she finally had the strength

To bring it into the light

And now that question

Never spoken

Embedded deep within her soul

Found the courage

To form on her lips

'Who am I?

Why am I here?'

And she watched

As the wind carried her words away

To a destination unknown

What if our intuition isn't this soft and gentle voice within?

What if it is a strong and demanding presence

That we have locked away deep inside of us

In fear of what she is commanding us to do?

#mellysthestorycollector

Lightning made shadows dance in the dark

Torrential rain fell like bullets on her skin

The mighty trees bowed and broke

Ripped from the earth

Their roots laid bare

As the storms power

Lashed out with bitter vengeance

No options left

Nowhere else to turn

Only one choice remained

She must abandon her home

And leave the wild behind

It was time to seek refuge

In the darkness

Of the cave

I feel like the universe itself

Has me in its grasp

Squeezing the life out of me

Taking away all my choices

Until I have no other options

But to surrender to its mercy

And it hurt

To acknowledge

The limits of her strength

The self-reliance

So hard acquired

Now being bent and broken

By something

Entirely outside of her control

The storm outside

Continued for days on end

Taunting her

Mocking her

Daring her to step back into its vicious onslaught

It grew in anger at her refusal to heed

Changing angles

Tactics

Mercilessly trying to reach her

Uproot her

Break her

Day after day

Night after night

Forcing her deeper and deeper

Into the cave

Deeper and deeper

Into the depths of darkness

I can't take it anymore

It hurts too much

I feel it too deeply

And while I am strong

Even this is testing my limits

It hurts too much

To face reality

To face what is really happening

So I choose not to

I choose to hide within myself

And wait

This pain must end at some point

Right?

Etched into an impassable cliff face

The cave sat forebodingly

At the edge of the forest

Sinisterly inviting

With its thick lush ferns

Growing around a trickle of water

Leaking from somewhere

Deep within the darkness

But within that blackness

There were places the light could not touch

A whisper

Murmur

From within its depths

That chilled her to the very bone

Forcing her to look over her shoulder

Into the endless night behind her

I don't want to be here

It's uncomfortable

Dark

Lonely

But how can I go back

And face that reality?

I have no choice but to stay here

And wait for it to end out there

Come to me

        me

          me

A voice echoed

Words rippling

From within the darkness

She could not see her

The owner of this voice

But she could feel her

A presence there in the dark

Justifying the uneasy feeling

Firmly settled within her gut

Come to me

      me

        me

I will show you

      Show you

        Show you

What you seek

      Seek

        Seek

A cool breeze wrapped itself around her

Tingling her skin

Her own voice heard

Echoing on its formless shape

Who am I?

Who am I?

Who am I?

Come to me

     me

       me

I will show you

     Show you

       Show you

What you seek

     Seek

       Seek

I'm scared to step further inwards

But I must seek out this thing within me

There is something waiting for me

And in spite of this darkness

I will find it

I must

I have to

I need answers

With one final glance

To the raging storm at her back

She stepped blindly

Into the oppressive darkness before her

Darkness all around her

Suffocating

Restricting

Pulling her into its depths

Every part of her being wants to fight

Resist

Struggle

Escape this space

Go back to the light

Sink deeper

    deeper

    deeper

Let it happen

    happen

    happen

Allow it to consume you

    consume you

    consume you

Surrender to the darkness

    the darkness

    the darkness

    ...Surrender to me

Hopelessness

Moving through the dark

Directionless

Aimless

No sight

To prove she had moved forward

No sign posts

To show how far she had come

Just the endless night of hopelessness

Void of stars

I'm tired

So tired

I'm moving

But what if I'm going in circles?

What if I'm getting nowhere?

This is hopeless!

And yet

I've come so far

To give up now

I must go on

But onto what?

How?

Where?

What do I do now?

Closing her eyes

The voice returned

No longer an echo

But still just a murmur

Vibrating within the endless night

It will take silence and stillness

To face what lies ahead

And only in facing this

Can you find what you seek

So she waited patiently

In the stillness

Of her own mind

For what was yet to come

The silence within her

Merged with the silence of the cave

No longer aware of where she ended

And the cave begun

It is time

Open your eyes

See the magic

Unfolding around you

Little by little

The cave came to life

Glow worms nestled into the ceiling

Creating stars above her head

Reflecting off pools of water

Trickling through the rocks

Tufts of green marking their edges

Little sprigs of soft hope

Emerging from the hardness of the cave floor

So much beauty hiding here

Nestled comfortably in the dark

So much happening

Right here in the stillness within me

Why have I never noticed it before?

Exploring

Curious

Lost in wonder

At the world within

Goosebumps on her neck

Breathless

Scared

Eyes watching her

Lurking in the dark

Layering of voices

Hissing from the walls

Uneasy feeling

Creeping up her spine

Not alone anymore

We've been waiting for you

We've been waiting for you

We've been waiting for you

We've been waiting for you

We've been waiting for you

We've been waiting for you

We've been waiting for you

We've been waiting for you

We've been waiting for you

Fear tells her to run

Escape

Avoid at all costs

But her heart overrides

Locking her feet in place

I cannot run

I must face this

For the answer to my question

Is greater than my fear

I feel the earth beneath me

And allow her strength to rise within me

I feel the blood pumping through my veins

And allow the strength of my ancestors to rise within me

I feel my fast beating heart

And allow it to ignite the flames of our combined strength

I call it forth

Your strength

Our strength

My strength

I will face this

Together

They surrounded her

Dark figures

Coming to life

From the cave walls

Monsters

Distorted

Twisted

All bearing a face

That mirrored her own

See us

Hear us

Know us

Feel the truth

They circled her

Snarling

Hissing

Clawing at her

Invading her space

Trying to tear her down

So she pushed back

Refusing to remain the prey

Of their sick and twisted game

The figures vanished instantly

Whispers of ghosts

Visiting here in the dark

Their evil grins

Etched into her mind

Their overlaying voices

Lingering in the air

Why do they have my face?

Why do they look like me?

How do I face...

myself?

It will take silence and stillness

To face the distortions of your minds

And only in facing the messengers of your darkest self

Can you find what you seek

Don't fight them

Face them

See them

Hear them

Know them

Know you

In

Out

Sitting still

In the dark

Listening to her own breath

In

Out

Determination rising

A desire to overcome

To succeed

In

Out

Toes pushing into the cave floor

Feeling the earths whispering support

Stable and forever secure

In

Out

Feeling the strength of her ancestors

The Wild Women before her

Standing with her always

In

Out

Hearing the dark ones

Impatiently rustling in the space

Between her breaths

In

Out

Deep sighing breath

Calling for them

To join her

Strike

Flame

Sizzle

Burn

The first of the monsters

Sat before her

Hair covering her face

The essence of contempt

Rolling from her in heavy waves

Strike

Flame

Sizzle

Burn

One by one she played with matches

Staring only at the flame

Burning it down

Snuffed out where flame met twisted flesh

Strike

Flame

Sizzle

Burn

Strike

Flame

Sizzle

Burn

Tension hung in the air

Haunted by the smell of burning flesh

Both waiting for the other to make a move

While the monster continued

Her little painful game

Strike

Flame

Sizzle

Burn

Skin crawling

From reflected pain

Not her own

As she screamed at the monster to stop

Its head shot upwards

Revealing a vicious snarl

Etched into a face that was entirely her own

Why should I?

You've never cared enough to stop me before

Eyes locked in defiant stares

Flashes of herself

Where she too had worn this snarl

Mirrored in the monsters eyes

Moments where she had lit the match

Just to watch the world burn

Even if it meant

Hurting herself in the process

This was a reflection of her own self-destruction

This monster was her

How many times have I worn this face

Completely unaware

Of the damage it was causing?

How many matches have I lit

Completely unaware

Of the people I was hurting?

How many more times must I do it

Before I am no longer unaware?

Pulling back from the sea of memories

She truly saw the monster before her

A reflection of herself

A princess in rebellion

Wanting to be seen and heard

Not by others

But by herself

I'm sorry

I'm sorry I didn't see you

I'm sorry I didn't hear you

I'm sorry you had to hurt yourself

Over and over again

Trying to get my attention

I'm sorry for the pain this caused

The pain I caused us

I'm sorry

Better to feel the pain

At your own hands

Than to leave others

Holding a dagger to your heart

Tears poured down her face

As she realised the sacrifice

This dark one had made for her

This monster

This young woman before her

Had protected her heart

From the pain others would inflict on her

Time and time again

She stood between her heart and others

A battering ram for the abuse

That would have shattered her then fragile heart

How many times?

How many times have I

Expected others to hurt me

And instead hurt myself first?

When will I learn the lesson

And stop hurting myself

In fear of what may come?

Breathe catching in her chest

As her walls of protection

Began to crumble

Feeling

For a fraction of a second

The magnitude of the pain

This poor monster had held back from her

It's time to stop protecting my heart

From a fictional pain

That may never come

It's time to take responsibility

For my own twisted behaviour

It's time to stop relying on this

Unconscious form of myself

To bear the brunt of this pain

Like a tangled ball of yarn

Once wrapped around itself ever so tightly

She pulled at the loose thread in her mind

And watched as it began to unravel

I'm sorry my lack of responsibility

Has caused you so much pain

My little monster

I thank-you for protecting me

Oh so very many times

And most importantly,

I love you for doing this.

Her walls of protection shattering

Piece by piece

Falling to the floor

She swept the monsters distorted form

Her form

Into her loving embrace

And to her surprise

The dark one

This monster

This twisted reflection

Softened

Quietened

Relaxed

And hugged her back

All the monsters in her mind came

Stepping out of the darkness

Waiting for their turn to speak

No longer viewed with fear

But now a compassionate curiosity

An eagerness to uncover

What truths she had hidden from herself

One by one

She spoke with them

Her Monsters

Her Dark Ones

Her Unconscious Behaviours

Grabbing them by the shoulders

Drawing them in closely

Wrapping them in her warm embrace

And showing them the love

They so truly deserved

Thank-you all so much

For everything you have done for me

You my rebellious self-destruction monster

For protecting my heart from pain

You my manipulative perfectionist monster

For showing me what I desire

And even you my bitter angry monster

For showing me what I value

I'm sorry it has taken me so long to see you

I'm sorry I left you in the dark for so long

But I see you now

And I promise I will forever more.

I love you.

No longer monsters

Simply darker parts of herself

Beautiful

And very dearly loved

Do you see us now?

Do you hear us now?

Do you know us now?

Can you feel us now?

Yes

I understand now

My darker feelings, words and actions

Are the way you speak to me

A way to show me

Where my heart is hurting

Where my desires are not being honoured

Where my values are being disregarded

And I must take responsibility for these

In order to release you from the burden

Of unconscious protection

Do you see you now?

Do you hear you now?

Do you know you now?

Do you understand now?

I must have a dark side

Monsters

Dark Ones

In order to be whole

I cannot run from them

Ignore them

Or push them away

For in doing so

I push away a fundamental part of myself

I must love them

ALL of them

For to do so

Is to love me

ALL of me

Emotionally raw

Vulnerable

Open

Unprotected

And yet

The strongest she had ever been

Outside the cave

Day turned to night

Night turned to day

Everyday life continued

Unaware of the journey

Going on inside of her

Your journey is not yet over, Child

You have embraced the darkness

As your path to the light

But it is time to embrace the light

For now it can be born from the darkness

Her monsters gathered around her

Pushing her

Pulling her

Towards the direction of the voice

Once this feeling would have scared her

But now there was no fear

For she knew they were not trying to hurt her

She now understood their purpose

And although twisted at times

They always came from a place of love

The space was tight

Too tight

It took her breathe away

With each push forward

Each pull from her monsters

The cave walls

Hugging her in a too strong embrace

Biting at her skin

She had come this far

She was not giving up now

No matter how uncomfortable this felt

With no walls

To protect her heart from pain

No expectations

Of her monsters to do this for her

She felt every jab

Every nick

Every moment of self-doubt

Like a dagger through her heart

Every moment of self-judgement

Like boiling water on her skin

This voice within me

Filled with promises

Is asking too much

Too soon

I already feel raw

Vulnerable

Exposed

This is too much

What if she isn't

What I think she is?

What if she is leading me

To my own destruction?

It is not me you fear

But the consequences of my commands

For I ask you to leave comfort behind

And to follow me into the unknown

Right

Left

Right

Right

Duck under

Step up

She followed

To a place

Where even the life

Inside the cave

Dare not shine

And her monster fell behind

I'm so close

I can feel it deep within my bones

But there's something different

About this part of the cave

The dark is getting darker

The air feels heavier

Harder to move through

Like an invisible wall

I have to push through

The darkness pressed in on her

Squeezing her tighter and tighter

Hard to breathe

Heart beating fast

No one to protect her

Flight and fight activated

Struggling to suck in the air

Her burning lungs needed

Fight it

Breath

Survive

Surrender to the darkness

Allow it to take over you

You will feel like you are suffocating

In the darkness of your own soul

But there you will remember

What you are

Who you are

Why you are

And as you remember

You will take your first breath

It will feel like you are dying

For Child, a part of you is

The wall you have created

To protect yourself from the truth

Is being cleansed

Dissolved into nothingness

You are dying

So you may be reborn

In your pure truth

With lungs burning

Her body weak

From the constant fight

For survival

She just let go

In the absence of protection

Long built around her heart

The truth rang loud and clear

Finally making itself known

All my life I have been holding back

In fear of my own pain

My own emotions

My own power

Why would I limit myself?

I'm not holding back anymore

From myself

From life

I've spent so long choosing my pain

Choosing my emotions

Instead of choosing my power

But no more

I choose me

Last of strength

Voice booming

Echoing over and over

Directed at the unseen voice

Invisible in the darkness

ENOUGH!

    ENOUGH!

        ENOUGH!

            ENOUGH!

                ENOUGH!

                    ENOUGH!

                        ENOUGH!

The power in her command

Shook the cave around her

The walls releasing her

From its too tight grip

Freeing her

To breathe

To stand

To live

Enough!

I will not tolerate this pain anymore

This horrible game of cat and mouse

I do not deserve to be treated this way

I deserve to be treated with respect

And from this point on

If you want me to follow you

Then you will do as I command!

Light as bright as day

Filled the cave

A dark figure standing in the middle

A crown resting upon her head

A vision of respect

Authority

Sovereignty

Standing tall and proud

Emanating the light around her

And as her eyes adjusted

She realised this figure before her

Wore a face

That mirrored her own

You are ready

You will now step forward as your true self

You will be all that you can be

You will allow yourself to remain free and true

You will always follow the call of your heart

You will be guided by the wisdom of the past

You will rule yourself with truth and respect

Doing what is right for you always

It is time to embrace your light

The Dark Queen smiled

With compassionate strength

Removing the crown

Placing it on her head

A symbol of the transference

Of power

That had always been within her

The crown felt solid

Weighty

Making her stand taller

Prouder

Becoming the vision of strength

That stood before her

Tears streamed down her face

A mix of joy

Triumph

Achievement

But also, an overwhelming sadness

For how long it had taken her

To finally reclaim

The part of herself

That was always rightfully hers

How could I forget you?

Forget me?

Forget my power?

How could I forget my own sovereignty?

Have you seen

What you are?

Do you accept

What you are?

Will you be

What you are?

I am a Queen

I will not suffer those who are not worthy of me

I will not fight for anyone's attention

You will follow me because I demand respect

For myself

For others

For all

I am a Queen

I will not tame or deny

All that I am

My monsters serve me

My wild side serves me

My nurturer serves me

My determination serves me

I am a Queen

I honour all that I am

My emotions

My feelings

My actions

My wisdom

My intentions

I am a Queen

I am worthy

I am deserving

Of greatness

Of love

Of power

Of light

The Queen placed her hand between her breasts

Her touch rippling through her body

An overwhelming feeling of being whole

Washed over her

And she watched in awe

As the light that filled the cave

Began to flow through the Queens hand

And into her own heart

I'm coming home

To me

To my highest potential

To all I am destined to be

Its time

To open myself to all my soul wants for me

To open my heart to the abundance of life

To say goodbye to fear

Self doubt

Self destruction

Self judgement

Its time to radiate as the full essence of all that I am

Unrestrained

Wild

Limitless

Powerful

Its time to be me

As the light flowed

From one to the other

The Dark Queen's voice

Began resonating within her

No longer a whisper

Hiding deep within the darkness

But strong and guiding

Right at the surface of her mind

Seated firmly in the steady beating of her heart

Do you see now?

Do you hear now?

Do you know now?

Do you understand?

Tell me, Child

Who are you?

I am both monster

And miracle.

I am light.

I am dark.

I am Princess.

I am Mother Goddess.

I am Wild Woman.

I am Queen.

But above all else,

I am worthy of giving

And receiving all that life has to offer me.

As the light transferred

From one to the other

Slowly the Queen began to fade

But she did not feel a loss

Of the powerful woman before her

For she could feel the Queen's love

Compassionate strength

Commanding presence

Radiating from within her

No longer denying

The truth of her own sovereignty

And no longer separated

From the voice of intuition within her

Her own light shone brightly

You are ready now, Child

There is one more part of yourself

You have yet to meet

Who holds the answer to your final question

It's time to discover

Why you are here

It was then

For the first time

Since she had entered the darkness

She could see a clear path

To the light of dawn

Shining brightly

At the end of the cave

There comes this moment in our lives

That usually follows a period of darkness

A great epiphany

In which we see how powerful we truly are

#mellysthestorycollector

It was time

To step out of the darkness

Emerge from the cave

Full of light

Hope

Wonder

The darkness had served its purpose

Allowed her to go deeper than ever before

Find parts of herself that she did not know exist

But it was time to create from the light of life

It was time to be the light

Joyful

Wonderous

Alive

It was time to live

A deep sadness crept over her

A mourning for the end of a journey

That had given her so much insight

Into the depths of her own mind

But the sadness did not stay

For it was born out of gratitude

Love

Appreciation

Thankfulness

For all the darkness had given her

I release the past

I release the darkness

I release the heaviness

I claim my light

I claim my divine right

I claim my magic

Here and now

I claim me!

She saw life renewed

Through the lense of clear eyes

Witnessing magic everywhere

In the flap of a butterflies wings

In the swaying of the trees

In the sound of a childs laughter

She found joy and wonder in the miracle of life

And each held a message for her

Reminding her of just how powerful

Each and every being was

At their very core

But the world was loud now

Her time in the dark

Had made her sensitive to life

The sound of a bird in flight

Resounded like thunder in her ears

The sight of the setting sun

Burned images behind her eyelids

The feeling of the breeze on her skin

Tingled in ways reserved for her lovers

And while it made her mourn for the comfort

The quiet

The stillness

Of the dark she had left behind

She did not let her monsters wallow in the pity

For she knew she was meant to be in the light

And here is where she would stay

Step up

Accept

Allow

Surrender

I will allow the power within me to grow

Let it consume me

Overtake me

Become me

I am powerful

And I claim it

She held her breath

Waiting for life to reveal the next steps forward

But life itself

Held its breath waiting for her

An uncomfortable pause

Breathless stillness

A delicate dance

Of endless possibilities

Each waiting for the other

To make the first move

Planting her feet firmly in the ground

She looked to the sky

Felt the light within her shine brightly

And called on the ancients of her past to guide her forward

Ancient Ones,

Unlock the next part of my journey

As your flames of knowledge light my way

Pierce the illusions blocking my path

Show me my unlimited potential

Show me the possibilities of life

I am ready

Can you hear it?

The black raven calling

From atop the trees

'Be not afraid' it says

'Follow me

Destiny awaits'

Can you hear it?

The words under its sound

Vibrating out from your very heartbeat

'Answer my call' it says.

Following the ravens call

The Princess within

Danced for joy

Loving this newfound freedom

This new adventure

This new path

That life had presented her

She heard the women's cries

Long before she saw her

The unmistakeable sound

Of a woman's anguish

Pulling her forward

The Mother Goddess within her

Demanding she help

A fellow mother in pain

She sat and listened to her story

Held quiet space for the pain and anguish

To flow out of the woman

Such a simple gesture

That meant so much to both

This poor woman has been through so much

If only she could see what I can

The bigger pattern playing out in her life

The reason and purpose behind it all

If only she could see what I can

That this is the beginning of her journey

That she, too, will step into her Wild Woman

Unleash the bitterness locked within her heart

And find that connection she is so desperately seeking

If only she could know what I know

'It all happens for a reason.'

Such simple words to say

But ones that cut deep

When invalidating the pain

Of the present

The quiet gentle space between them

Instantly warped and twisted

Tension hanging in the air

As the tears she had been trying to soothe

Ran even harder and more bitter than before

The essence of pain hanging unsaid between them

What just happened?

I was trying to help her

Give her a glimmer of hope

I was just trying to help her

What did I just do?

Do not dishonour her journey

By minimising her pain

For how can she rise from it

If she can't feel its presence?

While her intentions had been pure

The hurt she had caused another

Cut deeply

Apologies not enough

To heal the fresh pain

Caused by her own hand

Do not be hard on yourself, Child

Sometimes

You will be the bad guy

In another's story

A necessary catalyst

For their own journey

Do not be sorry for the role you play

For while it is heavy

It is also an honour

Bestowed upon very few

With the Dark Queen's words

Ringing in her ears

She gave herself space

And retreated into nature

To heal her own pain

Mother Earth,

I sat with you today

Pushed my toes into your earth

The grass blades under my fingertips

Your breath whispering in the wind

I sat with you today

Shared with you my thoughts and pain

Felt your energy wrap around me

Healing me

Clearing me

Holding me

I sat with you today

Felt my tension and fears fade away

Your love fill me from head to toe

Found myself renewed by your presence

I sat with you today

And remembered I was home

I was safe

And I was forever loved

Renewed by the Mother Goddess' love

Self-forgiveness lingering in her heart

She continued on her journey

Confidence oozing from her very being

The sensual magnetism of her inner power

Now vibrating through to her outer world

All those she passed knew

This was a woman who loved life

But for some

A woman loving life

Is a reflection

Of all they lack

A target for the uncomfortableness

Festering within them

They threw their insecurities at her

Like a Princess throwing bombs

Desperately deflecting all they saw in her

That they wished they had in themselves

Desperately trying to drag her down

For their own comfort

But little did they know

You cannot break someone

Who has risen from the flames

Of their own destruction

It's interesting how fiercely

They keep trying to drag me down

My mere presence

Now an affront

To their very existence

Do I speak my mind?

Tell them they have crossed my boundaries

Stand up for my self-respect

Self-beliefs

Self-love

But is there more self-respect in walking away

Especially when I know their words

Come from their own pain?

Some people will never change

Will never allow themselves

To hear your words

No matter how loud

You speak

Wish them well

But let them go

For it is their journey

Not yours

They could not destroy her

No matter how hard they tried

But she could feel the pressure

Of their attempts

As the disconnect

Between other's journeys

And her own

Grew wider

She found herself alone again

Not quite belonging to the world of men anymore

For she knew more than she could say

And so much more than they were ready to hear

I don't want to hurt anyone

But there is so much I can say

To help those around me

But how can I do that

When they are afraid

Of my very existence?

Maybe its better if I just keep my power to myself

Keep my words to myself

Keep my light to myself

If I shine too brightly

I could hurt others

But after everything

I don't want to live in fear either

I've earned the right to shine

Haven't I?

Why was she doing that?

Holding her voice back

Swallowing that lump in her throat

Still playing small for the comfort of others

Even after everything she had been through

Why?

When her heart was aching to say how it felt

When her mind longed to share what it knew

When her soul ached to express its joy

Why?

Why was she still letting the world dictate her life

Why did she still feel less than whole?

But most importantly,

Why was she still letting them

Make her feel this way?

I just want to be free

To say what is in my heart

Mind

Soul

I just want to be me.

ALL OF ME!

Help me please!

How do I do this?

How do I be all of me

In a world that is uncomfortable

With those who shine brightly?

A hot shiver ran up her spine

The sense of being surrounded

By comfort and support

Feeling all of herself there

Princess

Mother Goddess

Wild Woman

Dark Queen

Surrounding her

Filling her

With their love

They call you names

Like Bitch or Witch

Because they are afraid of you

But they do not know why

They see your strength

A power from deep within

That no one will ever control

And they fear what they can not control

So they call you names

In hate

In fear

Out of their own jealousy

They wish they had your strength

Your knowledge

Your power

But they do not yet seek the awareness

Required to obtain it

The journey of discovering your magic is not an easy one

It means diving deeper into yourself

Each and everyday

Exploring the darkest corners

Of your mind

Your soul

Your heart

And then finding comfort and solace there

But this is what makes you strong

Your willingness to go where others won't

So let them call you what they will

Hold your head high with pride

For it honours the strength you hold within

And the power at your fingertips

For you ARE the Sorceress

And darling Child...

Well darling you are Magical

The lessons of the Princess

The Mother Goddess

The Wild Woman

The Dark Queen

All began to glow

Crystal clear in her mind

With the epiphany of awareness

All of it

Has been bringing me to here

Right here

To this moment

Where I can

Once and for all

Become all of who I am

Where I can

Once and for all

Accept the magic within me

I may not be able to control

How others receive my magic

Because they will always see it

From the stage of self they are at

The truth is

It's not about them

It's about me

I owe it to myself to be consistent

I owe it to myself to be disciplined

I owe it to myself to be focussed

I owe it to myself to be all of who I am

This is the final part of myself

I am a Sorceress.

I have the power at my fingertips

To create

To destroy

To allow growth

Or to facilitate death

But I choose how I wield this power

For it is my magic

It is me

Finally whole

All of herself present

She wrote the code

By which she would live her life

I have no control over others behaviour

Or their reactions to mine

But I can control my own

And use the wisdom of my journey

To show them compassion

Empathy

Understanding

When they respond from a place of pain

I will honour the fact that

Although I want to help others

Especially those in pain

I must be patient

Stay in my own magnetism

And allow those who need me

To ask for my help

In their own time

In their own space

In their own way

Its only then can I wield

All that I am to help them

For it is their journey

And I am but a catalyst

Along their path

I accept and respect

The duality and polarity of life

Nothing is ever black or white

Good or evil

Right or wrong

These are but two extremes

Of the whole

And at times

The pendulum must swing

Just as my emotions do

Before centre

Before truth

Can be found

There will be times when I must exert my will

Use my natural electricity to go get what I want

And there will be times when I must allow things to come to me

Use my natural magnetism to attract all that I desire

I honour and respect these two forces

Within myself

Within others

Within nature

Within the universe

For we are neither one nor the other

But electromagnetic beings

Living in a world of endless possibilities

Like a leaf

Falling on the surface of water

I am conscious of the ripples

I send out into the world

For every action I take

Or do not take

Every thought I think

Or do not think

Every feeling I feel

Or do not feel

Causes a reaction elsewhere

I will be mindful of this

As I step lightly through life

I am complete

Whole

Full

Just as I am

Right here

Right now

In every single moment

Of everyday

I am always

And will forever more

Be complete

A divine being

Born of stardust

Always connected to the stars

With the magic of my ancestors

And the universe

Running through my veins

I honour and accept the fact

My journey is never truly finished

That at any given moment

On any given day

My monsters may take over

I may be drawn into the darkness

My Wild Woman may scream in anger

My emotions may become uncontrollable

And my Princess may demand her freedom

When this happens

I will be kind to myself

And move through the stages

With ease and grace

Knowing that each move made

Each step presented to me

Is for my own evolution

Until I once again remember

Just how powerful I truly am

Until I remember

I am

And always will be

The Sorceress

She fell to her knees

The sheer magnitude of power

Flowing through her

Taking her breath away

Body vibrating

With the energy of the earth

Flowing through her

Body vibrating

With the universal energy

Flowing through her

Body vibrating

As these energies mixed

With her own

Creating a new

But potent mix of energy

That was her very own

'I see you Sorceress'

Said the Princess within

'I love you Sorceress'

Said the Mother Goddess within

'I honour your strength Sorceress'

Said the Wild Woman within

'I respect your power Sorceress'

Said the Dark Queen within

Feeling the support

Within her

Under her

Around her

She rose

Fully

Completely

Accepting the power

Of her sorcery

Her power

Herself

My purpose is now clear

If I am to live my life by these codes

Fully supported by the truths

That resonate with each Stage of Self

Then there is only one way

I can impact the world consciously

Compassionately

Kindly

... I must be the example for others to follow

It was time to begin again

Voice strong

Confident

Connected

Allowing the truth to flow through

Declaring how her life would be

In every moment of every day

Claiming it

Living it

Loving it

It was time to show the world

Exactly who she was

With her magic

Leading the way

She watched as the young girl sat crying

The group she had just been playing with

Isolating her

Teasing her

Pushing her away

She sat next to her quietly on the bench

Saying nothing for quite some time

Allowing the safety of her energy

To overflow into the girl's presence

Finally, the girl turned to look at her

Forcing a small smile to cross her face

Skin blotchy

Nose running

Eyes still swollen from the tears

She smiled back kindly at the girl

'Would you like to hear a story

About a Princess

Who learned to rescue herself?'

I know you think your purpose in life is to do something

But it is so much more than that

Your purpose is to BE all of who you are

What you choose to do with that...

... is entirely up to you.

#mellysthestorycollector

Stepping Forward

For some of you, this is where our journey together ends, and I trust these pages have served you well. But if you are not ready for our time together to end just yet, here are some ways I can support you going forward:

Stages of Self Membership Program

The Stages of Self Membership Program gives you the educational understanding behind the poetry. This self-paced program allows you to step through the stages of self in a different way, gaining a deeper understanding as you do, while supported by a fast growing community of women who understand exactly where you are at.

Sorceress 1:1 Mentoring

For those who are ready to jump headfirst into their own journey, the Sorceress 1:1 Mentoring is a 11-week intensive into your own Stages of Self. Together we explore how these cycles are playing out in all areas of your life and find practical, measurable action steps to move you ever closer to standing in your full Sorceress power.

Stages of Self Accreditation Program

Are you a coach, mentor or intuitive and would love to incorporate the Stages of Self methodology into your own business? The Stages of Self Accreditation Program gives you the training, tools and resources you need to support your clients through their own Stages of Self.

www.MellyS.com.au

About the Author

Melly Stewart is a Women's Personal and Business Development Author, Speaker, Trainer, Facilitator & Mentor, Intuitive Tarot Reader, and Award-Winning Nature Photographer. She is the author of *Stages of Self: Your Journey to Self-Empowerment*, creator of the *5 Stages of Self* Methodology, and as a self-proclaimed Story Collector, hosts the *#courage1000project* WebTV & Podcast.

Influenced by the research of Brené Brown and the written works of Elizabeth Gilbert, Melly Stewart has used her 10+ years' experience in Photography & Videography, 15+ years in the entrepreneurial space, 18+ years in various forms of Customer Service (along with her highly intuitive and curious nature) to develop a unique methodology to help modern women find their own way to self-empowerment.

Her mission is to provide education, community and guidance to spiritually minded women who are ignoring their own needs due to the pressures of everyday life. She helps them solve this by taking them through their own Stages of Self, showing that Personal or Business... it all starts with *you*.

<u>www.mellys.com.au</u>

About the Lightcodes

Victoria Pirini is an Intuitive Guide that specialises in helping women reconnect with their purpose and power through readings, channelling and Lightcodes for both personal and business use.

There's no mucking around with Victoria's codes as they are here to help you to step into your power and own your gifts and abilities. Her symbols are for those people ready to commit to themselves and share their magick with world.

Her Lightcodes work by activating the energy that is currently lying dormant within your very soul. Upon seeing them, you begin to feel its message as your body and soul shift to re-awaken and align with this energy.

<u>www.victoriapirini.co</u>

Thank-you

To those women who have done the work before me.

Thank-you for paving a path for me to follow.

I love you.

To those women in my life who chose not to go on this journey.

Thank-you for showing me the importance of why it must be done.

I love you.

To those women who are walking the path with me.

Thank-you for standing with me as we go on this magical ride together.

I love you.

To those women who have yet to discover the path.

I am waiting for you with open arms.

I love you.